50 Flavorful Curry Recipes from Around the Globe

By: Kelly Johnson

Table of Contents

- Thai Green Curry
- Indian Butter Chicken
- Jamaican Goat Curry
- Malaysian Laksa Curry
- Japanese Katsu Curry
- Vietnamese Coconut Curry
- Ethiopian Berbere Curry
- Pakistani Karahi
- Sri Lankan Fish Curry
- South African Bunny Chow
- Caribbean Curry Shrimp
- Nepalese Chicken Tarkari
- Bangladeshi Beef Curry
- Indonesian Rendang
- Burmese Khow Suey
- Trinidadian Curry Duck
- Kenyan Nyama Choma Curry
- Cambodian Amok Curry
- Afghan Lamb Qorma
- Iranian Khoresh
- Moroccan Tagine Curry
- Maldivian Fish Curry
- Fijian Coconut Curry
- Singaporean Fish Head Curry
- Filipino Kare-Kare
- Mauritian Octopus Curry
- Indian Chickpea Chana Masala
- Indian Paneer Tikka Masala
- Indian Lamb Rogan Josh
- Indian Prawn Malai Curry
- Thai Massaman Curry
- Thai Panang Curry
- Indian Egg Curry
- Indian Keema Curry
- Indian Vegetable Korma

- Bangladeshi Shorshe Ilish
- Indonesian Soto Ayam
- Indian Daal Makhani
- Indian Madras Curry
- South Indian Chettinad Curry
- Vietnamese Lemongrass Curry
- Japanese Vegetable Curry
- Thai Jungle Curry
- Indian Vindaloo
- South Indian Sambhar
- Malaysian Kapitan Chicken Curry
- Ethiopian Doro Wat
- Caribbean Curry Crab
- Indian Malabar Prawn Curry
- Burmese Eggplant Curry

Thai Green Curry

Ingredients:

For the curry paste:

- 3 green chilies (adjust to taste)
- 2 shallots, chopped
- 4 garlic cloves
- 1-inch piece of ginger or galangal
- Zest of 1 lime
- 2 stalks of lemongrass (white part only)
- 1 cup fresh cilantro (stems included)
- 1 tsp ground coriander
- 1 tsp ground cumin
- 1 tbsp fish sauce (or soy sauce for vegetarian)
- 2 tbsp coconut milk

For the curry:

- 2 tbsp vegetable oil
- 400g (14 oz) chicken breast or tofu, cut into bite-sized pieces
- 1 cup green beans, trimmed
- 1 red bell pepper, sliced
- 1 zucchini, sliced
- 400ml (14 oz) coconut milk
- 1 cup chicken or vegetable stock
- 1 tbsp fish sauce or soy sauce
- 1 tsp sugar
- 1 handful Thai basil leaves
- Juice of 1 lime

Instructions:

1. Make the curry paste:
Blend all the curry paste ingredients in a food processor or blender until smooth. Set aside.

2. Cook the curry:
Heat the vegetable oil in a large pan or wok over medium heat. Add the curry paste and cook for 2–3 minutes, stirring constantly, until fragrant.

3. Add protein:
Add the chicken or tofu to the pan and cook for 5 minutes, coating it with the paste.

4. Add vegetables:
Stir in the green beans, bell pepper, and zucchini. Cook for 2–3 minutes.

5. Simmer the curry:
Pour in the coconut milk and stock. Add fish sauce (or soy sauce) and sugar. Stir well and let simmer for 10–15 minutes until the vegetables are tender.

6. Finish the dish:
Remove from heat and stir in Thai basil and lime juice.

7. Serve:
Serve hot over jasmine rice or rice noodles. Garnish with extra basil or cilantro, if desired.

Indian Butter Chicken

Ingredients:

For the marinade:

- 500g (1 lb) boneless chicken thighs, cut into chunks
- 1 cup plain yogurt
- 1 tbsp lemon juice
- 1 tbsp garam masala
- 1 tsp turmeric powder
- 1 tsp chili powder
- 1 tsp salt

For the curry:

- 2 tbsp butter
- 1 tbsp oil
- 1 large onion, finely chopped
- 4 garlic cloves, minced
- 1-inch piece of ginger, minced
- 2 tsp garam masala
- 1 tsp ground cumin
- 1 tsp ground coriander
- 1 cup tomato purée
- 1 cup heavy cream
- 1 tsp sugar
- Salt to taste
- Fresh cilantro, chopped

Instructions:

1. **Marinate the chicken:**
   Mix all the marinade ingredients. Add the chicken, coat well, and marinate for at least 1 hour (or overnight).
2. **Cook the chicken:**
   Heat oil in a pan and sear the chicken until golden brown on all sides. Remove and set aside.
3. **Make the curry:**
   In the same pan, melt butter, then sauté onions until golden. Add garlic, ginger, garam masala, cumin, and coriander, cooking until fragrant.

4. **Simmer**:
   Add tomato purée and simmer for 10 minutes. Stir in cream, sugar, and salt.
5. **Combine**:
   Add the chicken back into the pan and cook for another 10–15 minutes.
6. **Serve**:
   Garnish with cilantro and serve with naan or rice.

Jamaican Goat Curry

Ingredients:

- 1 kg (2 lbs) goat meat, cubed
- Juice of 1 lime
- 2 tbsp Jamaican curry powder
- 2 tsp ground allspice
- 1 tsp salt
- 2 tbsp vegetable oil
- 1 large onion, chopped
- 4 garlic cloves, minced
- 1 Scotch bonnet pepper, chopped (adjust for spice level)
- 2 medium potatoes, peeled and cubed
- 2 cups coconut milk
- 2 cups water
- 1 tsp thyme
- 2 green onions, chopped

Instructions:

1. **Prepare the meat**:
   Rinse the goat meat with lime juice. Season with curry powder, allspice, and salt.
2. **Brown the meat**:
   Heat oil in a large pot and brown the goat meat in batches. Set aside.
3. **Cook the aromatics**:
   In the same pot, sauté onions, garlic, and Scotch bonnet until fragrant.
4. **Simmer**:
   Add the browned goat meat, coconut milk, water, thyme, and green onions. Cover and simmer for 1.5–2 hours until tender.
5. **Add potatoes**:
   Stir in the potatoes and cook for another 20–30 minutes until soft.
6. **Serve**:
   Serve hot with rice and peas or roti.

Malaysian Laksa Curry

Ingredients:

For the laksa paste:

- 5 red chilies
- 3 garlic cloves
- 2-inch piece of ginger
- 2 lemongrass stalks (white part only)
- 2 tsp ground coriander
- 1 tsp turmeric powder
- 1 tbsp shrimp paste
- 1 tbsp oil

For the curry:

- 200g (7 oz) rice noodles
- 1 tbsp oil
- 400ml (14 oz) coconut milk
- 4 cups chicken or seafood stock
- 200g (7 oz) shrimp or chicken
- 1 cup bean sprouts
- 1 boiled egg, halved
- 1 lime, quartered
- Fresh cilantro and mint, for garnish

Instructions:

1. **Make the laksa paste:**
   Blend all paste ingredients until smooth.
2. **Cook the paste:**
   Heat oil in a pot, then sauté the laksa paste until fragrant.
3. **Simmer the broth:**
   Add coconut milk and stock. Simmer for 10 minutes.
4. **Cook the protein:**
   Add shrimp or chicken to the broth and cook until done.
5. **Prepare noodles:**
   Cook rice noodles according to package instructions and divide them into bowls.

6. **Assemble**:
   Pour the curry broth over the noodles. Top with bean sprouts, egg, lime, and fresh herbs.
7. **Serve**:
   Serve hot with extra lime wedges on the side.

Japanese Katsu Curry

Ingredients:

For the curry:

- 2 tbsp vegetable oil
- 1 onion, finely chopped
- 2 garlic cloves, minced
- 1-inch piece of ginger, minced
- 2 tbsp curry powder
- 1 tbsp flour
- 2 cups chicken stock
- 1 tbsp soy sauce
- 1 tbsp honey
- 1 carrot, sliced
- 1 potato, cubed

For the katsu:

- 4 chicken breasts
- Salt and pepper, to taste
- 1 cup flour
- 2 eggs, beaten
- 1 cup panko breadcrumbs
- Oil for frying

Instructions:

1. **Make the curry:**
   Heat oil in a pan, sauté onion, garlic, and ginger until soft. Add curry powder and flour; cook for 1 minute. Gradually add chicken stock, stirring until smooth. Add soy sauce, honey, carrot, and potato. Simmer for 20 minutes until thickened.
2. **Prepare the katsu:**
   Season chicken breasts with salt and pepper. Dredge in flour, dip in beaten eggs, and coat with panko breadcrumbs. Deep-fry until golden and cooked through.
3. **Serve:**
   Slice the chicken and serve over steamed rice with curry sauce poured on top.

Vietnamese Coconut Curry

Ingredients:

- 2 tbsp vegetable oil
- 1 onion, sliced
- 3 garlic cloves, minced
- 1-inch piece of ginger, minced
- 2 tbsp red curry paste
- 1 lb chicken or tofu, cubed
- 1 cup coconut milk
- 1 cup chicken or vegetable stock
- 1 sweet potato, cubed
- 1 red bell pepper, sliced
- 1 tbsp fish sauce or soy sauce
- Juice of 1 lime
- Fresh cilantro for garnish

Instructions:

1. **Cook aromatics**:
   Heat oil in a pot, sauté onion, garlic, and ginger until fragrant. Stir in curry paste.
2. **Add protein and vegetables**:
   Add chicken or tofu, sweet potato, and bell pepper. Stir to coat.
3. **Simmer**:
   Add coconut milk, stock, and fish sauce. Simmer for 20 minutes until everything is cooked through.
4. **Finish**:
   Stir in lime juice and garnish with cilantro. Serve over rice or noodles.

Ethiopian Berbere Curry

Ingredients:

- 2 tbsp vegetable oil
- 1 onion, chopped
- 4 garlic cloves, minced
- 1-inch piece of ginger, minced
- 2 tbsp berbere spice mix
- 1 lb beef or chicken, cubed
- 2 cups tomatoes, chopped
- 1 cup water or broth
- 1 cup lentils (optional)
- Salt to taste

Instructions:

1. **Cook aromatics:**
   Heat oil, sauté onion, garlic, and ginger. Add berbere spice and toast briefly.
2. **Add protein and liquid:**
   Stir in meat, tomatoes, and water. Add lentils if using. Simmer for 30–40 minutes.
3. **Serve:**
   Serve with injera or rice.

Pakistani Karahi

Ingredients:

- 2 tbsp ghee or oil
- 1 lb chicken, cut into pieces
- 2 tomatoes, chopped
- 1 tsp ginger-garlic paste
- 1 tsp red chili powder
- 1 tsp garam masala
- 1 tsp cumin seeds
- Salt to taste
- Fresh cilantro and ginger juliennes for garnish

Instructions:

1. **Cook chicken**:
   Heat ghee, fry chicken until lightly browned.
2. **Add spices and tomatoes**:
   Add ginger-garlic paste, spices, and tomatoes. Cook until chicken is tender and sauce thickens.
3. **Serve**:
   Garnish with cilantro and ginger. Serve with naan.

Sri Lankan Fish Curry

Ingredients:

- 1 lb firm white fish, cubed
- 1 onion, sliced
- 3 garlic cloves, minced
- 1 tbsp curry powder
- 1 cup coconut milk
- 1 cup water
- 1 tsp turmeric powder
- 1 tbsp tamarind paste
- Curry leaves

Instructions:

1. **Cook aromatics:**
   Sauté onion, garlic, and curry leaves. Add spices and tamarind.
2. **Simmer:**
   Add coconut milk and water. Bring to a simmer.
3. **Add fish:**
   Add fish cubes and cook until done.
4. **Serve:**
   Serve with rice or roti.

South African Bunny Chow

Ingredients:

- 2 tbsp oil
- 1 onion, chopped
- 2 garlic cloves, minced
- 1 lb lamb or beef, cubed
- 2 tbsp curry powder
- 2 tomatoes, chopped
- 1 cup stock
- 1 loaf of bread, hollowed out

Instructions:

1. **Cook curry**:
   Heat oil, sauté onion and garlic. Add meat, curry powder, and tomatoes. Simmer with stock until tender.
2. **Assemble**:
   Fill the hollowed-out bread with curry.
3. **Serve**:
   Serve hot, tearing bread to scoop curry.

Caribbean Curry Shrimp

Ingredients:

- 1 lb shrimp, peeled
- 2 tbsp oil
- 1 onion, chopped
- 2 garlic cloves, minced
- 1 tbsp curry powder
- 1 cup coconut milk
- 1 bell pepper, sliced
- 1 Scotch bonnet pepper, minced

Instructions:

1. **Cook aromatics:**
   Sauté onion, garlic, and curry powder.
2. **Simmer:**
   Add coconut milk, bell pepper, and Scotch bonnet. Cook shrimp until done.
3. **Serve:**
   Serve with rice.

Nepalese Chicken Tarkari

Ingredients:

- 2 tbsp ghee
- 1 lb chicken, cut into pieces
- 1 onion, chopped
- 3 garlic cloves, minced
- 1-inch ginger, minced
- 1 tsp turmeric
- 1 tsp cumin
- 1 cup tomatoes, chopped
- 1 cup stock

Instructions:

1. **Cook aromatics:**
   Heat ghee, sauté onion, garlic, and ginger. Add spices.
2. **Simmer:**
   Add chicken, tomatoes, and stock. Simmer until tender.
3. **Serve:**
   Serve with rice or flatbread.

Bangladeshi Beef Curry

Ingredients:

- 1 lb beef, cubed
- 2 tbsp mustard oil
- 2 onions, finely chopped
- 4 garlic cloves, minced
- 1-inch ginger, minced
- 2 tomatoes, chopped
- 2 tsp ground coriander
- 1 tsp ground cumin
- 1 tsp turmeric
- 1 tsp garam masala
- 2 green chilies, chopped
- 1 cup beef stock
- Salt to taste
- Fresh cilantro for garnish

Instructions:

1. **Cook aromatics**:
   Heat mustard oil in a large pot. Sauté onions until golden. Add garlic, ginger, and green chilies; cook until fragrant.
2. **Add spices**:
   Add ground coriander, cumin, turmeric, and garam masala. Stir well.
3. **Brown beef**:
   Add beef cubes, searing them on all sides.
4. **Simmer**:
   Add chopped tomatoes and beef stock. Stir, cover, and simmer for 1–1.5 hours until beef is tender.
5. **Serve**:
   Garnish with fresh cilantro. Serve with steamed rice or paratha.

Indonesian Rendang

Ingredients:

- 2 lbs beef, cubed
- 2 tbsp vegetable oil
- 1 onion, chopped
- 4 garlic cloves, minced
- 1-inch ginger, minced
- 1 stalk lemongrass, smashed
- 2 kaffir lime leaves
- 2 tbsp curry powder
- 1 can (14 oz) coconut milk
- 1 cup beef stock
- 2 tbsp soy sauce
- 1 tbsp palm sugar or brown sugar
- 2-3 red chilies, chopped (optional)
- Salt to taste

Instructions:

1. **Cook aromatics**:
   Heat oil in a large pot. Sauté onion, garlic, and ginger until softened.
2. **Add beef and spices**:
   Add beef cubes, lemongrass, kaffir lime leaves, curry powder, and red chilies. Stir well.
3. **Simmer**:
   Add coconut milk, beef stock, soy sauce, and palm sugar. Stir, bring to a simmer, and cook on low heat for 1.5–2 hours until beef is tender and sauce thickens.
4. **Serve**:
   Serve with steamed rice.

Burmese Khow Suey

Ingredients:

- 1 lb chicken or tofu, cubed
- 2 tbsp oil
- 1 onion, chopped
- 4 garlic cloves, minced
- 1-inch ginger, minced
- 2 tbsp curry powder
- 1 can (14 oz) coconut milk
- 2 cups chicken or vegetable stock
- 2 tbsp soy sauce
- 1 tbsp fish sauce
- 1 tsp sugar
- 2 tbsp lime juice
- Boiled egg noodles
- Garnishes: boiled eggs, fried onions, chopped cilantro, lime wedges, chili oil

Instructions:

1. **Cook aromatics:**
   Heat oil in a pot. Sauté onion, garlic, and ginger until softened.
2. **Add chicken or tofu:**
   Add chicken (or tofu) and cook until browned.
3. **Add curry powder and liquids:**
   Stir in curry powder, coconut milk, chicken stock, soy sauce, fish sauce, and sugar. Bring to a boil, then reduce to a simmer. Cook for 15 minutes.
4. **Serve:**
   Serve over boiled egg noodles and garnish with boiled eggs, fried onions, cilantro, lime, and chili oil.

Trinidadian Curry Duck

Ingredients:

- 1 lb duck, cut into pieces
- 2 tbsp curry powder
- 1 onion, chopped
- 4 garlic cloves, minced
- 1-inch ginger, minced
- 2 tbsp oil
- 1 scotch bonnet pepper, chopped (optional)
- 2 tbsp soy sauce
- 2 tbsp vinegar
- 1 cup chicken stock
- 2 potatoes, cubed
- Fresh cilantro for garnish

Instructions:

1. **Marinate duck:**
   Coat duck pieces with curry powder, salt, and half the ginger, garlic, and scotch bonnet. Let marinate for at least 30 minutes.
2. **Cook duck:**
   Heat oil in a large pot. Brown duck on all sides.
3. **Add vegetables and liquids:**
   Add onion, garlic, ginger, and scotch bonnet. Sauté for 3 minutes. Add soy sauce, vinegar, chicken stock, and potatoes.
4. **Simmer:**
   Cover and cook on low heat for 1–1.5 hours until duck is tender and sauce thickens.
5. **Serve:**
   Garnish with fresh cilantro. Serve with rice or roti.

Kenyan Nyama Choma Curry

Ingredients:

- 1 lb beef or lamb, cubed
- 2 tbsp vegetable oil
- 1 onion, chopped
- 2 garlic cloves, minced
- 1-inch ginger, minced
- 2 tbsp curry powder
- 1 can (14 oz) diced tomatoes
- 1 cup beef stock
- 1 tsp turmeric
- 1 tbsp soy sauce
- 1 tbsp lemon juice
- Fresh cilantro for garnish

Instructions:

1. **Brown the meat**:
   Heat oil in a pot and brown the meat.
2. **Add aromatics and spices**:
   Add onion, garlic, ginger, and curry powder. Sauté until fragrant.
3. **Simmer**:
   Add diced tomatoes, beef stock, turmeric, soy sauce, and lemon juice. Cover and simmer for 45 minutes until meat is tender.
4. **Serve**:
   Garnish with cilantro. Serve with rice or flatbread.

Cambodian Amok Curry

Ingredients:

- 1 lb fish (such as catfish or tilapia), cut into chunks
- 1 can (14 oz) coconut milk
- 1 onion, chopped
- 2 tbsp red curry paste
- 2 tbsp fish sauce
- 1 tbsp sugar
- 1 tbsp lime juice
- 2 eggs
- 1 stalk lemongrass, smashed
- 3 kaffir lime leaves
- Fresh basil and cilantro for garnish

Instructions:

1. **Prepare the curry sauce:**
   In a blender, combine coconut milk, red curry paste, fish sauce, sugar, and lime juice. Blend until smooth.
2. **Simmer fish:**
   In a pot, combine the curry sauce with lemongrass, kaffir lime leaves, and fish chunks. Simmer for 10-15 minutes.
3. **Add eggs:**
   Beat eggs and add to the curry mixture, stirring gently. Simmer until eggs are cooked.
4. **Serve:**
   Garnish with fresh basil and cilantro. Serve with rice.

Afghan Lamb Qorma

Ingredients:

- 1 lb lamb, cubed
- 2 tbsp ghee
- 1 onion, finely chopped
- 3 garlic cloves, minced
- 1-inch ginger, minced
- 1 tbsp ground coriander
- 1 tsp ground cumin
- 1 tsp ground cinnamon
- 1 cup yogurt
- 2 tbsp tomato paste
- 2 cups water
- Salt to taste
- Fresh cilantro for garnish

Instructions:

1. **Cook lamb:**
   Heat ghee in a pot. Brown lamb pieces on all sides.
2. **Add aromatics and spices:**
   Add onion, garlic, and ginger. Cook until softened. Add coriander, cumin, and cinnamon.
3. **Simmer:**
   Stir in yogurt, tomato paste, and water. Simmer for 45 minutes to 1 hour until lamb is tender.
4. **Serve:**
   Garnish with fresh cilantro. Serve with naan or rice.

Iranian Khoresh

Ingredients:

- 1 lb chicken or beef, cubed
- 2 tbsp vegetable oil
- 2 onions, chopped
- 4 garlic cloves, minced
- 1 tsp turmeric
- 1 tbsp tomato paste
- 1 can (14 oz) chickpeas, drained
- 1 cup water or broth
- 1 tsp cinnamon
- 1 tbsp sugar
- Salt to taste

Instructions:

1. **Cook meat**:
   Heat oil in a pot and brown the meat. Remove and set aside.
2. **Cook onions and spices**:
   Sauté onions, garlic, and turmeric until fragrant. Add tomato paste and cook for 1-2 minutes.
3. **Add liquids and simmer**:
   Add chickpeas, water, cinnamon, and sugar. Return meat to the pot and simmer for 45 minutes.
4. **Serve**:
   Serve with rice.

Moroccan Tagine Curry

Ingredients:

- 1 lb chicken or lamb, cubed
- 2 tbsp olive oil
- 1 onion, chopped
- 3 garlic cloves, minced
- 1 tbsp ground cumin
- 1 tbsp ground cinnamon
- 1 tsp turmeric
- 1 can (14 oz) diced tomatoes
- 1 cup chicken or vegetable stock
- 1 cup dried apricots, chopped
- Salt and pepper to taste
- Fresh cilantro for garnish

Instructions:

1. **Cook aromatics:**
   Heat olive oil in a tagine or pot. Brown the meat, then remove. Sauté onion and garlic until softened.
2. **Add spices and liquids:**
   Add cumin, cinnamon, turmeric, diced tomatoes, stock, and apricots. Stir and bring to a simmer.
3. **Simmer:**
   Return the meat to the pot and simmer for 45 minutes until tender.
4. **Serve:**
   Garnish with fresh cilantro. Serve with couscous.

Maldivian Fish Curry

Ingredients:

- 1 lb fish (such as tuna or snapper), cut into pieces
- 1 tbsp vegetable oil
- 2 onions, chopped
- 4 garlic cloves, minced
- 1-inch ginger, minced
- 2 tomatoes, chopped
- 1 tsp turmeric
- 1 tsp ground coriander
- 1 tsp chili powder
- 1 cup coconut milk
- 1 cup water or fish stock
- 1 tsp tamarind paste
- Salt to taste
- Fresh cilantro for garnish

Instructions:

1. **Cook aromatics**:
   Heat oil in a large pot. Sauté onions, garlic, and ginger until softened.
2. **Add spices**:
   Add turmeric, coriander, and chili powder. Stir well.
3. **Cook the fish**:
   Add chopped tomatoes and cook for 2 minutes. Add fish, coconut milk, water, and tamarind paste.
4. **Simmer**:
   Simmer for 15-20 minutes until the fish is cooked through and the curry thickens.
5. **Serve**:
   Garnish with fresh cilantro. Serve with rice.

Fijian Coconut Curry

Ingredients:

- 1 lb chicken or lamb, cut into pieces
- 1 tbsp vegetable oil
- 1 onion, chopped
- 2 garlic cloves, minced
- 1-inch ginger, minced
- 2 tomatoes, chopped
- 1 can (14 oz) coconut milk
- 1 cup chicken stock
- 1 tsp curry powder
- 1 tsp ground turmeric
- 2 tbsp soy sauce
- 1 tsp sugar
- Salt to taste
- Fresh cilantro for garnish

Instructions:

1. **Cook aromatics**:
   Heat oil in a large pot. Sauté onion, garlic, and ginger until softened.
2. **Add spices**:
   Stir in curry powder, turmeric, and tomatoes. Cook for 2 minutes.
3. **Cook protein**:
   Add chicken (or lamb) to the pot and brown the pieces.
4. **Add liquids and simmer**:
   Add coconut milk, chicken stock, soy sauce, and sugar. Stir well and simmer for 20–30 minutes until the protein is tender.
5. **Serve**:
   Garnish with fresh cilantro. Serve with rice.

Singaporean Fish Head Curry

Ingredients:

- 1 fish head (usually snapper), cut into pieces
- 2 tbsp vegetable oil
- 2 onions, chopped
- 4 garlic cloves, minced
- 1-inch ginger, minced
- 2 tbsp curry powder
- 1 can (14 oz) coconut milk
- 1 cup chicken stock
- 1 eggplant, chopped
- 1 tomato, chopped
- 1 red chili, chopped
- 1 tbsp tamarind paste
- Salt to taste
- Fresh cilantro for garnish

Instructions:

1. **Cook aromatics**:
   Heat oil in a large pot. Sauté onions, garlic, and ginger until softened.
2. **Add curry powder and vegetables**:
   Stir in curry powder, eggplant, tomato, and chili. Cook for 2 minutes.
3. **Simmer the curry**:
   Add coconut milk, chicken stock, and tamarind paste. Bring to a simmer.
4. **Add fish head**:
   Add fish head pieces and cook for 15–20 minutes until the fish is tender.
5. **Serve**:
   Garnish with cilantro. Serve with rice.

Filipino Kare-Kare

Ingredients:

- 1 lb oxtail or beef shank, cut into pieces
- 2 tbsp vegetable oil
- 2 onions, chopped
- 4 garlic cloves, minced
- 1 tsp ground rice flour
- 1 cup peanut butter
- 1 eggplant, sliced
- 1 banana blossom (optional), sliced
- 1 bunch of bok choy or banana heart, chopped
- 4 cups beef stock
- 1 tbsp fish sauce
- 1 tsp salt
- Fresh shrimp paste (bagoong) for serving

Instructions:

1. **Brown the oxtail:**
   Heat oil in a large pot. Brown oxtail pieces on all sides.
2. **Cook aromatics:**
   Add onions, garlic, and cook until softened. Stir in ground rice flour and peanut butter.
3. **Simmer the curry:**
   Add beef stock and fish sauce. Stir well and simmer for 1–1.5 hours until the meat is tender.
4. **Add vegetables:**
   Add eggplant, banana blossom, and bok choy. Cook for 5–7 minutes until tender.
5. **Serve:**
   Serve with shrimp paste on the side. Enjoy with rice.

Mauritian Octopus Curry

Ingredients:

- 1 lb octopus, cleaned and cut into pieces
- 2 tbsp vegetable oil
- 1 onion, chopped
- 4 garlic cloves, minced
- 1-inch ginger, minced
- 2 tomatoes, chopped
- 1 tbsp curry powder
- 1 tsp turmeric
- 1 can (14 oz) coconut milk
- 1 cup water
- 1 tbsp soy sauce
- Salt to taste
- Fresh cilantro for garnish

Instructions:

1. **Cook aromatics**:
   Heat oil in a large pot. Sauté onion, garlic, and ginger until softened.
2. **Add spices**:
   Stir in curry powder and turmeric. Cook for 2 minutes.
3. **Cook octopus**:
   Add octopus pieces and cook for 5 minutes, stirring to coat in spices.
4. **Simmer**:
   Add tomatoes, coconut milk, water, and soy sauce. Stir well and simmer for 30–40 minutes until the octopus is tender.
5. **Serve**:
   Garnish with fresh cilantro. Serve with rice.

Indian Chickpea Chana Masala

Ingredients:

- 2 cups cooked chickpeas (or 1 can, drained)
- 2 tbsp vegetable oil
- 1 onion, chopped
- 4 garlic cloves, minced
- 1-inch ginger, minced
- 2 tomatoes, chopped
- 2 tsp ground cumin
- 2 tsp ground coriander
- 1 tsp garam masala
- 1 tsp turmeric
- 1 tsp chili powder
- 1 cup water
- Salt to taste
- Fresh cilantro for garnish

Instructions:

1. **Cook aromatics**:
   Heat oil in a large pan. Sauté onion, garlic, and ginger until softened.
2. **Add spices and tomatoes**:
   Stir in cumin, coriander, garam masala, turmeric, and chili powder. Cook for 2 minutes.
3. **Cook chickpeas**:
   Add tomatoes, chickpeas, and water. Stir well and simmer for 10–15 minutes.
4. **Serve**:
   Garnish with cilantro. Serve with rice or naan.

Indian Paneer Tikka Masala

Ingredients:

- 1 lb paneer, cubed
- 1 cup yogurt
- 1 tbsp ginger-garlic paste
- 1 tbsp lemon juice
- 2 tbsp vegetable oil
- 1 onion, chopped
- 2 tomatoes, chopped
- 1 tsp ground cumin
- 1 tsp ground coriander
- 1 tsp garam masala
- 1 tsp turmeric
- 1 cup cream
- Salt to taste
- Fresh cilantro for garnish

Instructions:

1. **Marinate paneer**:
   Mix yogurt, ginger-garlic paste, lemon juice, and a pinch of salt. Marinate paneer for 30 minutes.
2. **Cook the curry**:
   Heat oil in a pan. Sauté onions until softened. Add tomatoes and cook until mushy. Stir in cumin, coriander, garam masala, and turmeric.
3. **Add paneer**:
   Add the marinated paneer and cook for 5 minutes.
4. **Finish the curry**:
   Add cream and simmer for 10 minutes.
5. **Serve**:
   Garnish with fresh cilantro. Serve with naan or rice.

Indian Lamb Rogan Josh

Ingredients:

- 1 lb lamb, cut into pieces
- 2 tbsp vegetable oil
- 2 onions, chopped
- 4 garlic cloves, minced
- 1-inch ginger, minced
- 1 tbsp ground coriander
- 1 tbsp ground cumin
- 1 tbsp garam masala
- 1 tsp ground cinnamon
- 2 tomatoes, chopped
- 1 cup yogurt
- 1 cup water
- Salt to taste
- Fresh cilantro for garnish

Instructions:

1. **Brown lamb**:
   Heat oil in a pot. Brown lamb pieces on all sides.
2. **Cook aromatics**:
   Add onions, garlic, and ginger. Cook until softened. Stir in coriander, cumin, garam masala, and cinnamon.
3. **Add liquids**:
   Add tomatoes, yogurt, and water. Stir well and simmer for 1-1.5 hours until the lamb is tender.
4. **Serve**:
   Garnish with cilantro. Serve with rice.

Indian Prawn Malai Curry

Ingredients:

- 1 lb prawns, peeled and deveined
- 2 tbsp vegetable oil
- 1 onion, chopped
- 4 garlic cloves, minced
- 1-inch ginger, minced
- 2 tomatoes, chopped
- 1 can (14 oz) coconut milk
- 1 tbsp ground coriander
- 1 tbsp garam masala
- 1 tsp turmeric
- Salt to taste
- Fresh cilantro for garnish

Instructions:

1. **Cook aromatics:**
   Heat oil in a pan. Sauté onions, garlic, and ginger until softened.
2. **Add spices and tomatoes:**
   Stir in coriander, garam masala, turmeric, and chopped tomatoes. Cook until tomatoes soften.
3. **Add prawns and coconut milk:**
   Add prawns and cook for 5 minutes. Stir in coconut milk and simmer for 5 more minutes.
4. **Serve:**
   Garnish with cilantro. Serve with rice.

Thai Massaman Curry

Ingredients:

- 1 lb chicken or beef, cut into pieces
- 2 tbsp vegetable oil
- 1 onion, chopped
- 2 garlic cloves, minced
- 1-inch ginger, minced
- 1 tbsp Massaman curry paste
- 1 can (14 oz) coconut milk
- 1 cup chicken stock
- 2 potatoes, peeled and cubed
- 1 tbsp fish sauce
- 1 tbsp tamarind paste
- 1 tbsp sugar
- 1/2 cup roasted peanuts
- Salt to taste
- Fresh cilantro for garnish

Instructions:

1. **Cook aromatics:**
   Heat oil in a large pot. Sauté onions, garlic, and ginger until softened.
2. **Add curry paste:**
   Stir in Massaman curry paste and cook for 2 minutes.
3. **Add liquids:**
   Pour in coconut milk, chicken stock, fish sauce, tamarind paste, and sugar. Stir well.
4. **Simmer vegetables and protein:**
   Add potatoes and chicken (or beef). Simmer for 30-40 minutes until the meat is tender and the potatoes are cooked through.
5. **Finish and serve:**
   Stir in roasted peanuts. Garnish with fresh cilantro. Serve with rice.

Thai Panang Curry

Ingredients:

- 1 lb chicken or beef, cut into pieces
- 2 tbsp vegetable oil
- 2 tbsp Panang curry paste
- 1 can (14 oz) coconut milk
- 1/2 cup chicken stock
- 1 tbsp fish sauce
- 1 tbsp brown sugar
- 1 red bell pepper, sliced
- 1/2 cup basil leaves
- 1 tbsp lime juice
- Salt to taste

Instructions:

1. **Cook curry paste:**
   Heat oil in a pan. Add Panang curry paste and cook for 1-2 minutes to release the fragrance.
2. **Add liquids and protein:**
   Add coconut milk, chicken stock, fish sauce, and brown sugar. Stir well and bring to a simmer.
3. **Add vegetables and simmer:**
   Add chicken and red bell pepper. Simmer for 15-20 minutes until the chicken is cooked through.
4. **Finish and serve:**
   Stir in basil leaves and lime juice. Season with salt to taste. Serve with rice.

Indian Egg Curry

Ingredients:

- 6 boiled eggs, peeled
- 2 tbsp vegetable oil
- 1 onion, chopped
- 4 garlic cloves, minced
- 1-inch ginger, minced
- 2 tomatoes, chopped
- 1 tsp ground cumin
- 1 tsp ground coriander
- 1 tsp garam masala
- 1 tsp chili powder
- 1/2 cup water
- Salt to taste
- Fresh cilantro for garnish

Instructions:

1. **Cook aromatics:**
   Heat oil in a pan. Sauté onions, garlic, and ginger until softened.
2. **Add spices and tomatoes:**
   Stir in cumin, coriander, garam masala, and chili powder. Cook for 2 minutes. Add chopped tomatoes and cook until soft.
3. **Add eggs:**
   Add boiled eggs and stir gently. Pour in water and cook for 5-10 minutes to blend the flavors.
4. **Serve:**
   Garnish with fresh cilantro. Serve with rice or naan.

Indian Keema Curry

Ingredients:

- 1 lb ground lamb or beef
- 2 tbsp vegetable oil
- 1 onion, chopped
- 4 garlic cloves, minced
- 1-inch ginger, minced
- 2 tomatoes, chopped
- 1 tsp ground cumin
- 1 tsp ground coriander
- 1 tsp garam masala
- 1/2 tsp ground turmeric
- 1/2 cup peas (optional)
- 1 cup water
- Salt to taste
- Fresh cilantro for garnish

Instructions:

1. **Cook aromatics:**
   Heat oil in a large pan. Sauté onions, garlic, and ginger until softened.
2. **Brown the meat:**
   Add ground meat and cook until browned.
3. **Add spices and tomatoes:**
   Stir in cumin, coriander, garam masala, turmeric, and chopped tomatoes. Cook for 5-7 minutes.
4. **Simmer:**
   Add peas (if using) and water. Simmer for 15-20 minutes until the meat is tender and the curry thickens.
5. **Serve:**
   Garnish with fresh cilantro. Serve with rice or naan.

Indian Vegetable Korma

Ingredients:

- 2 tbsp vegetable oil
- 1 onion, chopped
- 4 garlic cloves, minced
- 1-inch ginger, minced
- 1 cup mixed vegetables (carrots, peas, potatoes, cauliflower)
- 1/2 cup cashew nuts
- 1/2 cup yogurt
- 1 tsp ground cumin
- 1 tsp ground coriander
- 1 tsp garam masala
- 1/2 tsp ground turmeric
- 1/2 cup cream
- Salt to taste
- Fresh cilantro for garnish

Instructions:

1. **Cook aromatics**:
   Heat oil in a large pan. Sauté onions, garlic, and ginger until softened.
2. **Add spices**:
   Stir in cumin, coriander, garam masala, and turmeric. Cook for 2 minutes.
3. **Add vegetables**:
   Add mixed vegetables and cook for 5-7 minutes.
4. **Make the sauce**:
   Blend cashew nuts with yogurt to form a smooth paste. Add this paste to the pan along with cream. Simmer for 15-20 minutes until the vegetables are tender.
5. **Serve**:
   Garnish with fresh cilantro. Serve with rice or naan.

Bangladeshi Shorshe Ilish

Ingredients:

- 1 lb hilsa fish (or any firm fish), cut into pieces
- 2 tbsp mustard oil
- 2 tbsp yellow mustard paste
- 2 green chilies, chopped
- 1 tsp turmeric
- 1 tsp ground cumin
- 1 tbsp ginger, minced
- 1 tomato, chopped
- 1/2 cup water
- Salt to taste

Instructions:

1. **Heat oil**:
   Heat mustard oil in a pan. Add fish pieces and fry them lightly for a few minutes. Remove and set aside.
2. **Cook aromatics**:
   In the same pan, add mustard paste, green chilies, turmeric, cumin, and ginger. Cook for 2 minutes.
3. **Add tomatoes and water**:
   Add chopped tomatoes and water. Stir well and cook until the tomatoes soften.
4. **Simmer fish**:
   Add the fried fish pieces back into the pan. Simmer for 10-15 minutes until the fish is cooked through.
5. **Serve**:
   Serve with rice.

Indonesian Soto Ayam

Ingredients:

- 1 lb chicken, whole or cut into pieces
- 2 tbsp vegetable oil
- 2 onions, chopped
- 4 garlic cloves, minced
- 1-inch ginger, minced
- 2 stalks lemongrass, smashed
- 4 kaffir lime leaves
- 1 tsp turmeric
- 1 tsp ground coriander
- 1 tbsp soy sauce
- 1 tbsp fish sauce
- 4 cups chicken broth
- Salt to taste
- Rice noodles or boiled eggs (optional)

Instructions:

1. **Cook aromatics:**
   Heat oil in a pot. Sauté onions, garlic, and ginger until softened.
2. **Add spices:**
   Stir in turmeric, coriander, lemongrass, and lime leaves. Cook for 2 minutes.
3. **Add chicken and broth:**
   Add chicken pieces and chicken broth. Bring to a boil, then simmer for 40-45 minutes until the chicken is cooked.
4. **Finish the soup:**
   Remove the chicken, shred it, and return it to the pot. Stir in soy sauce and fish sauce.
5. **Serve:**
   Serve with rice noodles, boiled eggs, and fresh herbs.

Indian Daal Makhani

Ingredients:

- 1 cup whole black lentils (urad dal)
- 1/4 cup kidney beans (rajma)
- 2 tbsp vegetable oil
- 1 onion, chopped
- 4 garlic cloves, minced
- 1-inch ginger, minced
- 2 tomatoes, chopped
- 1 tsp ground cumin
- 1 tsp ground coriander
- 1 tsp garam masala
- 1/2 tsp ground turmeric
- 1/2 cup cream
- Salt to taste
- Fresh cilantro for garnish

Instructions:

1. **Cook the lentils:**
   Soak the lentils and kidney beans overnight. Boil them in a pot until soft.
2. **Cook aromatics:**
   Heat oil in a pan. Sauté onions, garlic, and ginger until softened.
3. **Add spices and tomatoes:**
   Stir in cumin, coriander, garam masala, turmeric, and tomatoes. Cook until tomatoes soften.
4. **Combine and simmer:**
   Add the cooked lentils to the pan, along with some water. Simmer for 30 minutes. Stir in cream and cook for 10 more minutes.
5. **Serve:**
   Garnish with fresh cilantro. Serve with rice or naan.

Indian Madras Curry

Ingredients:

- 1 lb chicken or beef, cut into pieces
- 2 tbsp vegetable oil
- 1 onion, chopped
- 4 garlic cloves, minced
- 1-inch ginger, minced
- 2 tomatoes, chopped
- 1 tbsp Madras curry powder
- 1 tsp ground cumin
- 1 tsp turmeric
- 1/2 cup coconut milk
- 1 cup chicken broth
- Salt to taste
- Fresh cilantro for garnish

Instructions:

1. **Cook aromatics:**
   Heat oil in a pan. Sauté onions, garlic, and ginger until softened.
2. **Add spices and tomatoes:**
   Stir in Madras curry powder, cumin, turmeric, and chopped tomatoes. Cook until tomatoes soften.
3. **Add meat and liquids:**
   Add chicken or beef and cook until browned. Add coconut milk and chicken broth. Simmer for 30 minutes.
4. **Serve:**
   Garnish with fresh cilantro. Serve with rice or naan.

South Indian Chettinad Curry

Ingredients:

- 1 lb chicken or lamb, cut into pieces
- 2 tbsp vegetable oil
- 1 onion, chopped
- 2 tomatoes, chopped
- 4 garlic cloves, minced
- 1-inch ginger, minced
- 1 tsp cumin seeds
- 1 tsp fennel seeds
- 1 tsp black peppercorns
- 1 tbsp coriander powder
- 1 tbsp red chili powder
- 1/2 tsp turmeric powder
- 1/2 cup coconut milk
- 1/2 cup water
- Salt to taste
- Fresh curry leaves
- Fresh cilantro for garnish

Instructions:

1. **Dry roast spices**:
   In a dry pan, roast cumin, fennel seeds, and black peppercorns for 2-3 minutes until fragrant. Grind into a fine powder.
2. **Cook aromatics**:
   Heat oil in a pot. Sauté onions, garlic, and ginger until softened.
3. **Add spices and tomatoes**:
   Stir in coriander powder, chili powder, turmeric powder, and ground spices. Add chopped tomatoes and cook until soft.
4. **Cook meat**:
   Add chicken or lamb pieces and sauté until browned. Add water and coconut milk. Simmer for 25-30 minutes until the meat is tender.
5. **Finish**:
   Stir in fresh curry leaves and cook for a few more minutes. Garnish with fresh cilantro. Serve with rice or bread.

Vietnamese Lemongrass Curry

Ingredients:

- 1 lb chicken or tofu, cut into pieces
- 2 tbsp vegetable oil
- 2 stalks lemongrass, smashed
- 1 onion, chopped
- 2 garlic cloves, minced
- 1-inch ginger, minced
- 1 can (14 oz) coconut milk
- 1 cup vegetable stock
- 1 tbsp fish sauce
- 1 tbsp soy sauce
- 1 tbsp brown sugar
- 1 tbsp lime juice
- 1 red chili, sliced
- Fresh basil for garnish
- Salt to taste

Instructions:

1. **Cook aromatics**:
   Heat oil in a large pan. Add lemongrass, onion, garlic, and ginger. Sauté for a few minutes until fragrant.
2. **Add coconut milk and stock**:
   Pour in coconut milk, vegetable stock, fish sauce, soy sauce, and brown sugar. Bring to a simmer.
3. **Add protein**:
   Add chicken or tofu to the pan. Simmer for 20-25 minutes until the chicken is cooked or tofu is tender.
4. **Finish**:
   Stir in lime juice, sliced chili, and season with salt. Garnish with fresh basil. Serve with rice or noodles.

Japanese Vegetable Curry

Ingredients:

- 2 tbsp vegetable oil
- 1 onion, chopped
- 2 carrots, chopped
- 2 potatoes, peeled and chopped
- 1 cup cauliflower florets
- 1 zucchini, chopped
- 1 tbsp curry powder
- 1/2 tsp ground ginger
- 1/2 tsp ground turmeric
- 1 can (14 oz) coconut milk
- 2 cups vegetable broth
- 1 tbsp soy sauce
- 1 tbsp brown sugar
- Salt to taste
- Cooked rice for serving

Instructions:

1. **Cook vegetables**:
   Heat oil in a pot. Sauté onions until softened. Add carrots, potatoes, cauliflower, and zucchini. Cook for 5-7 minutes.
2. **Add spices**:
   Stir in curry powder, ginger, and turmeric. Cook for 2 minutes to release the spices' flavors.
3. **Add liquids**:
   Pour in coconut milk and vegetable broth. Bring to a simmer and cook for 20-25 minutes until the vegetables are tender.
4. **Finish**:
   Stir in soy sauce, brown sugar, and season with salt. Serve with rice.

Thai Jungle Curry

Ingredients:

- 1 lb chicken or beef, cut into pieces
- 2 tbsp vegetable oil
- 2-3 Thai bird's eye chilies, chopped
- 1 onion, chopped
- 4 garlic cloves, minced
- 1-inch ginger, minced
- 2 tbsp red curry paste
- 1 can (14 oz) coconut milk
- 1 cup chicken stock
- 1/2 cup bamboo shoots, sliced
- 1/2 cup bell peppers, sliced
- 1/2 cup Thai eggplant, sliced
- 1/4 cup fish sauce
- 1 tbsp lime juice
- Fresh basil for garnish
- Salt to taste

Instructions:

1. **Cook aromatics**:
   Heat oil in a pot. Add bird's eye chilies, onions, garlic, and ginger. Sauté for 3-4 minutes.
2. **Add curry paste**:
   Stir in the red curry paste and cook for 2 minutes until fragrant.
3. **Add liquids**:
   Pour in coconut milk, chicken stock, and fish sauce. Bring to a simmer.
4. **Add vegetables and protein**:
   Add chicken or beef, bamboo shoots, bell peppers, and Thai eggplant. Simmer for 20-25 minutes.
5. **Finish**:
   Stir in lime juice. Garnish with fresh basil. Serve with rice.

Indian Vindaloo

Ingredients:

- 1 lb pork or chicken, cut into pieces
- 2 tbsp vegetable oil
- 1 onion, chopped
- 4 garlic cloves, minced
- 1-inch ginger, minced
- 1 tbsp ground cumin
- 1 tbsp ground coriander
- 1 tbsp ground turmeric
- 1 tbsp paprika
- 2 tbsp vinegar
- 1 tbsp brown sugar
- 1 tbsp chili powder
- 1 can (14 oz) tomatoes, chopped
- 1/2 cup water
- Salt to taste
- Fresh cilantro for garnish

Instructions:

1. **Cook aromatics:**
   Heat oil in a pot. Sauté onions, garlic, and ginger until softened.
2. **Add spices:**
   Stir in cumin, coriander, turmeric, paprika, chili powder, and brown sugar. Cook for 2 minutes.
3. **Add meat and liquids:**
   Add pork or chicken and cook until browned. Add vinegar, tomatoes, and water. Bring to a simmer.
4. **Simmer:**
   Simmer for 30-40 minutes until the meat is tender and the sauce thickens.
5. **Serve:**
   Garnish with fresh cilantro. Serve with rice or naan.

South Indian Sambhar

Ingredients:

- 1 cup toor dal (yellow split peas)
- 2 tbsp tamarind paste
- 1 onion, chopped
- 1 tomato, chopped
- 1/2 cup mixed vegetables (carrot, pumpkin, beans)
- 1 tbsp sambar powder
- 1/2 tsp turmeric powder
- 1 tbsp mustard seeds
- 1 dried red chili
- 2 tbsp ghee (clarified butter)
- Fresh curry leaves
- Fresh cilantro for garnish
- Salt to taste

Instructions:

1. **Cook lentils:**
   Wash the toor dal and cook in a pot with water until soft and mushy. Set aside.
2. **Cook vegetables:**
   In another pot, add vegetables, tomatoes, and turmeric powder. Cook until the vegetables are tender.
3. **Prepare the tamarind base:**
   Dissolve tamarind paste in water and add to the pot with vegetables. Stir in sambar powder and bring to a simmer.
4. **Combine lentils and vegetables:**
   Add the cooked toor dal to the vegetable mixture. Simmer for 10-15 minutes.
5. **Prepare tempering:**
   In a small pan, heat ghee and add mustard seeds, dried red chili, and curry leaves. Once they splutter, pour this tempering over the sambhar.
6. **Serve:**
   Garnish with fresh cilantro. Serve with rice or idli.

Malaysian Kapitan Chicken Curry

Ingredients:

- 1 lb chicken, cut into pieces
- 2 tbsp vegetable oil
- 1 onion, chopped
- 4 garlic cloves, minced
- 1-inch ginger, minced
- 2 tbsp curry powder
- 1 tbsp ground turmeric
- 1 tbsp ground coriander
- 1 can (14 oz) coconut milk
- 1/2 cup chicken stock
- 2 tbsp tamarind paste
- 1 tbsp fish sauce
- 1 tbsp palm sugar (or brown sugar)
- 1 stalk lemongrass, smashed
- Fresh cilantro for garnish
- Salt to taste

Instructions:

1. **Cook aromatics**:
   Heat oil in a pot. Add onions, garlic, and ginger. Sauté until soft and fragrant.
2. **Add spices**:
   Stir in curry powder, turmeric, and coriander. Cook for 2-3 minutes until the spices are aromatic.
3. **Add chicken**:
   Add chicken pieces and cook until browned on all sides.
4. **Add liquids**:
   Pour in coconut milk, chicken stock, tamarind paste, fish sauce, and palm sugar. Stir well and add lemongrass.
5. **Simmer**:
   Bring to a boil, then reduce heat and simmer for 25-30 minutes until the chicken is cooked through and the sauce has thickened.
6. **Serve**:
   Garnish with fresh cilantro and serve with rice.

Ethiopian Doro Wat

Ingredients:

- 1 lb chicken drumsticks, skinless
- 2 tbsp vegetable oil
- 2 onions, chopped
- 4 garlic cloves, minced
- 1-inch ginger, minced
- 2 tbsp berbere spice mix
- 1 tsp ground turmeric
- 1 tbsp paprika
- 1 can (14 oz) tomatoes, chopped
- 1/2 cup chicken stock
- 4 hard-boiled eggs, peeled
- 1 tbsp niter kibbeh (Ethiopian spiced clarified butter)
- Salt to taste
- Fresh cilantro for garnish

Instructions:

1. **Cook onions:**
   Heat oil in a large pot. Add onions and sauté until golden and soft, about 10-12 minutes.
2. **Add spices:**
   Stir in garlic, ginger, berbere, turmeric, and paprika. Cook for 2-3 minutes.
3. **Add chicken:**
   Add chicken pieces and brown on all sides. Add tomatoes and chicken stock. Stir well.
4. **Simmer:**
   Cover and simmer for 30-40 minutes until the chicken is cooked through. Add the boiled eggs during the last 10 minutes of cooking.
5. **Finish:**
   Stir in niter kibbeh and salt to taste. Serve with injera or rice. Garnish with fresh cilantro.

Caribbean Curry Crab

Ingredients:

- 2 lbs crab, cleaned and cracked
- 2 tbsp vegetable oil
- 1 onion, chopped
- 2 garlic cloves, minced
- 1-inch ginger, minced
- 1 tbsp curry powder
- 1/2 tsp ground allspice
- 1 tbsp thyme (fresh or dried)
- 1 can (14 oz) coconut milk
- 1/2 cup chicken or seafood stock
- 1 scotch bonnet pepper, chopped (optional for heat)
- Salt and pepper to taste
- Fresh parsley for garnish

Instructions:

1. **Cook aromatics**:
   Heat oil in a large pot. Add onions, garlic, ginger, and scotch bonnet pepper. Sauté until soft and fragrant.
2. **Add spices**:
   Stir in curry powder, allspice, and thyme. Cook for 2-3 minutes.
3. **Add crab**:
   Add crab pieces and cook for a few minutes, turning to coat with the spices.
4. **Add liquids**:
   Pour in coconut milk and stock. Stir well.
5. **Simmer**:
   Cover and simmer for 20-25 minutes, ensuring the crab is cooked through and well-coated with the sauce.
6. **Serve**:
   Season with salt and pepper. Garnish with fresh parsley. Serve with rice or roti.

Indian Malabar Prawn Curry

Ingredients:

- 1 lb prawns, peeled and deveined
- 2 tbsp vegetable oil
- 1 onion, chopped
- 2 garlic cloves, minced
- 1-inch ginger, minced
- 1 green chili, chopped
- 1 tbsp ground coriander
- 1 tbsp ground cumin
- 1/2 tsp ground turmeric
- 1 can (14 oz) coconut milk
- 1/2 cup water
- 1 tbsp tamarind paste
- 1 tbsp fish sauce
- Fresh cilantro for garnish
- Salt to taste

Instructions:

1. **Cook aromatics**:
   Heat oil in a pan. Add onions, garlic, ginger, and green chili. Sauté until the onions are softened.
2. **Add spices**:
   Stir in coriander, cumin, and turmeric. Cook for 2 minutes until fragrant.
3. **Add liquids**:
   Pour in coconut milk and water. Stir in tamarind paste and fish sauce. Bring to a simmer.
4. **Add prawns**:
   Add prawns to the pan and cook for 5-7 minutes, until the prawns are pink and cooked through.
5. **Finish**:
   Season with salt to taste. Garnish with fresh cilantro. Serve with rice or paratha.

Burmese Eggplant Curry

Ingredients:

- 2 medium eggplants, chopped into bite-sized pieces
- 2 tbsp vegetable oil
- 1 onion, chopped
- 2 garlic cloves, minced
- 1-inch ginger, minced
- 1 tbsp ground turmeric
- 1 tbsp ground coriander
- 1 tbsp ground cumin
- 1 can (14 oz) tomatoes, chopped
- 1 cup vegetable broth
- 1 tbsp tamarind paste
- 1 tbsp soy sauce
- Fresh cilantro for garnish
- Salt to taste

Instructions:

1. **Cook eggplant**:
   Heat oil in a pan. Add eggplant pieces and cook until browned and tender. Remove and set aside.
2. **Cook aromatics**:
   In the same pan, add onions, garlic, and ginger. Sauté until soft and golden.
3. **Add spices**:
   Stir in turmeric, coriander, and cumin. Cook for 2 minutes.
4. **Add tomatoes and liquids**:
   Stir in tomatoes, vegetable broth, tamarind paste, and soy sauce. Bring to a simmer.
5. **Combine eggplant**:
   Return the eggplant to the pan. Simmer for 10-15 minutes until the curry thickens.
6. **Finish**:
   Season with salt to taste. Garnish with fresh cilantro. Serve with rice.

www.ingramcontent.com/pod-product-compliance
Lightning Source LLC
LaVergne TN
LVHW061950070526
838199LV00060B/4054